ON CREATIVE WRITING

LINDA A LAVID

REVIEWS FOR ON CREATIVE WRITING

Bitten by Book Lust Blog:

This quick to read book, was not only insightful, but helpful with tips I'd never seen explained so clearly. Her digestible dot points made noting and remembering the information easily and the book has given me a clear direction on how to briefly outline my own writing: staying focused and on track. Linda covers each short chapter from getting started to re-writing your work in a refreshing way. Overlooking heavy academic lectures for crisp to the point knowledge.

Goodreads:

A quick, compelling, and inspiring read for anyone who is a writer, wants to be, wishes they were, or thinks they can't become one. Lavid's background isn't in writing/grammar - which is refreshing - and her advice is practical. Read it.

The Compulsive Reader:

Employs gardening metaphors to take the reader from the planting of a seed, through watering, tending, filling the garden and digging the weeds. In terms of creating a piece of work, that translates into coming up with a good story idea and goal, creating plot, writing scenes, developing the story through elements like action, dialogue, and description, and finally rewriting. Lavid's simplified method is helpful and particularly valuable for newish or nervous authors.

Be wise.
Be prepared.
Dip your paddle straight down.
-Marjorie Norris

INTRODUCTION

ILLUSION IS THE FIRST OF ALL PLEASURES.
— OSCAR WILDE

Visualize . . .

Before you, I stand, a decidedly middle-aged woman, round, doughy, and blinking through smudged glasses. It's six p.m. We're in a VFW Post drinking bitter coffee from Styrofoam cups. I'm worried. It's my turn to disclose. All eyes, expectant, are on me. I clear my throat, swallow, then say, "My name is Linda — " I stop cold. What will you think? That I'm a fool, a loser? I want to run, but I've come this far. My confession tumbles out. "And I'm self-published."

A palling silence fills the air. I recoil, waiting for the jeers, the scoffs, and the room to empty. Remarkably, however, a voice calls out from the last row of seats (maybe it's yours), "Good evening, Linda." Relief sweeps through me. I am among friends . . . or at least one.

Backstory . . .

Thirty years ago, I embarked on writing the great American novel. At the time, I had completed an advanced degree and wanted another challenge. Writing a novel seemed like a good idea. It was an inexpensive undertaking for a single parent with young children and a full-time job. Certainly, I could steal moments in the early morning or during lunch. There was only one problem – I never demonstrated any particular writing talent. My worst subjects in high school were English and typing. Hardly portentous. But I was interested in the stories and foibles of human nature. So, with a sharpened pencil and a fresh pad, I took the plunge and began writing. In record time, however, I discovered that the subterranean world of creativity twisted darkly. I also learned I knew nothing, nada, zippo, about writing fiction. But I was up for the challenge – in the beginning.

I read books on writing and took copious notes. I deconstructed it to make the process understandable to myself. I struggled with tense and point of view and story . . . Well, um, it's about two sisters, and they have a friend who committed suicide. But it's a mystery. And they want to find out why it happened. I haven't entirely worked out the details or the beginning, but I know the end, and that's a start. I think . . .

Over the years, flashes of inspiration sparked then burned in roiling, despairing seas. I puzzled, avoided, and gave up too many times to remember. What kept me going? Certainly not accolades or desperate bidding wars for print rights. What kept me going was getting from point A to point B. It's about how to stay the course and not get lost. It's about what I've learned from writing fiction and publishing my work.

So, where am I today? My fiction has been used in college courses and published in award-winning journals. I have taught short story and novel writing classes and moderated writing groups. I've learned and grown, but most of all, I've taken charge not only of my writing but of the publishing and marketing of my work. Thanks to the technology of the 21st century, a golden era for writers is here.

The publishing world of the late 20th century was grim. Due to a couple of decades of diminishing returns and the buyout of many publishing houses, conglomerates heavily invested in an increasingly small pool of writers, who they tagged as "best selling," a self-fulfilling prophecy of their advertising dollars. To see this recurring truth, one only has to look at the New York Times bestseller list. But such is the way of the American free market, where products are branded, pumped, then sold to the masses. Not necessarily a bad thing. After all, John Grisham is very entertaining. The problem was it left many voices out of the mix.

Enter the equalizer – technology – and suddenly, the world, along with publishing, shifts. Computer technology, software, and the Internet have converged and dramatically changed the landscape for the independent writer. Every step, from writing to rewriting, book design to publishing, and marketing to selling, has changed the publishing paradigm. Manuscripts no longer need to languish on shelves or be sent dog-eared through the mail for another go-round with an agent or publisher. The waiting is over. A writer can now publish his work quickly and at a reasonable cost. Marketing outlets are infinite, given the virtual nature of the Internet, and never before has the relationship between writer and reader been so intimate. It's exciting. But with this freedom comes a huge responsibility to your readers and yourself. The task is daunting but hardly impossible. I somehow managed, taking one step at a time.

First and foremost, you must write the darn thing. This involves writing, rewriting, editing, head-bashing, then more of the same. Producing a book-length manuscript is hard work. In my case, it took years. There were several false starts – inching upwards, then sliding back – a steep learning curve. I began from the precarious position of having no training, formal or otherwise. I didn't have a clue. But I suspect most writers feel the same. How one writes or learns to write is tricky.

There are several aspects to writing fiction. Rendering what John Gardner in The Art of Fiction describes as a 'vivid and continuous dream' is a complicated affair. Story is created from a writer's imagination, who in turn must translate it onto a page of symbols so that another person can read, absorb, and similarly experience the story. It's a remarkable process when you think about it. So, are you up for the challenge, or is the writer's quintessential question nipping away inside: Do I have the talent?

We imagine talent as some vast reservoir of subconscious knowledge that some lucky people are born with. We think of Shakespeare and Mozart, and Einstein. But the truth is we all have talents of many kinds and measures. Think of your family and friends; assuredly, you can name many of their unique strengths. Talent is nothing more or less than individual ability. And while there are gifted writers, I do not believe having an innate talent is imperative to becoming an author.

Fiction demands a working knowledge of many points of craft. And while mastering craft can be daunting, each of us has skills to meet the challenge. If you have an analytical mind, cause and effect will be solid. If you are intuitive, your story will take imaginative twists. If you are emotional, you will have a true internal compass to tell a riveting story. If you are a global thinker, you will see the whole. If you are a detail person, your story will be tight. If you are a visual, auditory, or tactile person, your story will be vivid. If you are curious, writing will never bore you. If you are empathic, your characters will be believable. If you're old, you'll bring a wide array of experience into the process. If you're young, your story will be fresh. If you're stubborn and relentless, your story, at last, will be finished. So what's your talent? Most likely, you have many, some not even touched upon.

Before going further, I propose that writing can be taught and learned. I also submit that the quality you need most is neither talent nor knowledge but the mad, unrelenting desire to tell a story.

And with this passion, walk to the end of the diving board, loosen your shoulders, and take the plunge.

GETTING STARTED

So where do you put your toe in?

Backstory . . .

When I decided to write a novel, I had the impression that writing fiction would be easy, a winsome process that would fly on the wings of creativity. What fun to finally let go! As I'd mentioned, before tackling the craft of fiction, I had just come out of graduate school where, for three years, I had been entangled in writing academic papers that tended toward the dry and esoteric. So the thought of freeing myself from the objective to the subjective was exhilarating. Perhaps, looking back, my naiveté was a good thing. Otherwise, I wouldn't have started. It took me three years to complete my first book-length manuscript, that was unreadable in the clear light of day. During those early years, I did two things: I read books on writing, and I wrote. Neither was a bad thing, but besides taking an inordinately long time, I repeatedly made the same mistakes. And when it came time to rewrite, I didn't know where or how to start. The writing books were clear, concise, and redundant in what they had to say. I poured over them with gusto and did a lot of highlighting. But the wisdom that spewed forth never seeped into my brain for any practical purpose.

The tasks of writing and publishing are rife with fits and starts. Some aspects may come easily, while others will prove more trying. Looking back, I can now identify three critical activities that, once incorporated into my writing life, were and continue to be of immense help.

-Join a writer's group. In the absence of attending a writing program (an option not available to most of us), the advantages of joining a writer's group are tremendous. It is in this environment that craft can grow and flourish. Often, members in a group are diverse, not only in what they write but where they are on the writing-publishing-marketing continuum. Put all the members together, and a synergy occurs whereby a broad base of skill levels and experience can be freely shared. Besides having your writing reviewed, critiquing other people's work is helpful. Figuring out what works and why is a critical developmental step in learning how to write well. And there's also the commiseration factor. Like babies to new mothers, writing is fascinating to writers. Still, in the company of non-writers, such discussions may leave you standing alone, drink in hand, looking furtively at where your friendly listener disappeared. Writers' groups can be found in bookstores, continuing education programs, and online. It's been my experience that libraries have the space and are amenable to having community meetings. Membership can be open or restricted, receptive to all genres, or focused on a certain kind of writing. No matter how the group is configured, there's gold in 'them thar hills.'

-Write daily. Yeah. I avoided the daily quota for years: too much pressure, performance anxiety, fear of failure, you name it. Finally, one summer, I took on the challenge, stuck with a minimum of 250 words, and kept track of my daily progress. Some days I easily surpassed the quota. Writing daily keeps the story fresh and continuous. Start small if you like – one hundred words. Double that, and you'll have a novel-length manuscript in one year. It's crucial to choose a word-count quota that is doable and measurable. Be realistic, and don't set yourself up for failure. I also found Ernest Hemingway's advice helpful – keep water in the well. In other words, once you're done writing for the day, have a sense of where you'll be picking up the story the following day. For illustrative purposes, this paragraph runs 138 words.

-Analyze Story X. Immerse yourself in a novel or short story you wish you had written. I believe subconscious formatting occurs when a person reads, and the more one reads, the better she can write. There is also a state of natural selection, and what you hold up as your favorite book or story, most likely reflects the writing you want to take on. Immersion into a story is done by reading it, speaking it, and deconstructing it. To deconstruct, write an excerpt in long-hand and pay careful attention to words, sentences, paragraphs. As you develop craft, this book/story will hold many answers to your questions, i.e., How does the author handle description, backstory, transitions? My Story X is Margaret Atwood's The Robber Bride. I still marvel at how she plays with tense, description, and characterization. I have referred to this book endlessly in learning how to write. For example, when my characters were doing excessive walking, turning, and looking, I referred to a random page of Atwood's Bride and found some fixes. By the way, I do not write like Margaret Atwood... yet.

Before we hone in on craft, I have a commentary on writer's block. For years, writer's block was my nemesis.

Whenever I felt stupid or lazy or tired, whenever I couldn't find the time, made excuses, or gave up, I had writer's block. However, now I see the situation more clearly. Writer's block is simply a lack of craft, not having the basic writing concepts in place.

Now it's time to turn the page.

PLANT THE SEED ~ STORY GOAL

FICTION IS THE TRUTH WITHIN THE LIE.
— STEPHEN KING

*O*ur lives are full of creation. Awake or asleep, we forge ahead, forming, adjusting, trying it one way, then another. Creativity is embedded in who we are. And fiction is an extension of this creativity. No two stories will ever be the same, just as no two lives are the same. Every writer, every person, brings their unique perspective and talent to the party. I bristle whenever I hear there are no new stories, that everything written has been written before. Yes, there are general themes, but their execution will always be unique. Ask Manolo Blahnik about shoes and Valentino about dresses. But I digress.

So what in you craves expression? Maybe it's unfinished business you want to work out or a bit of human nature to explore. Having an idea for a story is very exciting. Your mind rushes with thoughts, images, and words fill the page. My God, you think, this is easy, this is effortless. I'm a genius. And maybe you are. On the other hand, you may be experiencing the first blush of wondrous inspiration, an interlude of sweet bliss. How wondrous it is, but oh so fragile. Now, I'm sure some writer in the history of humankind wrote a brilliant work on inspiration alone. However, this has not happened to me or any writer I know.

So you have an idea for a story. That's a very good thing. And maybe you even have a few pages of dialogue, narrative, and exposition. Wonderful. You're swimming in calm water, but decisions have to be made, and the sooner, the better – First, who is the story about?

"Well," you say, "it's about this girl and her mother and –"

"Stop. Who? Which one?"

"Both," you say. "It's a mother and daughter story and the conflicts they have."

"Hmm . . . How about some specifics? What's the daughter's name?"

"Mary."

"What does Mary want?"

"She wants to get away from her mother."

"What's stopping Mary from getting away?"

"She's been brainwashed. She isn't strong enough. Her mother is overpowering."

"Does Mary have the means to get away? Money, car, job?"

"No. They live together. Her mother supports her. Her mother holds all the cards. Mary's helpless."

"So the story is about a woman named Mary who wants to be out of her mother's home and away from her mother's controlling ways, but she doesn't have the means or the confidence to leave."

"Yes," you say. "Exactly."

"I love it!"

Every great story is about a character struggling. Every

great story mirrors our lives as we, too struggle. If strife were not a human condition, it wouldn't be the fabric of story-telling. To start a story in earnest, ask and answer these three questions in one declarative sentence: Who is my story about? What does this character want? What is stopping him from getting what he wants?

The declarative sentence from the above example is: The story is about a girl named Mary who wants to be out of her mother's home and away from her mother's controlling ways, but she doesn't have the means or the confidence to leave.

Story goal. This declarative sentence is also called the story goal. Think of story goal as the magnetic north. From page one until the end of your story, the story goal will be your homing device. It will keep your novel or short fiction piece focused and can even be used for publishing and marketing purposes. With some tweaking, you already have a blurb for your back cover!

Every story breaks down to this essential statement. But how can one sentence sum up a novel-length story? Consider Wally Lamb's 800-plus-page novel, I Know This Much Is True: An angry, resentful brother feels obligated to keep his schizophrenic twin out of harm's way. In Dan Brown's The Da Vinci Code: A man under suspicion must solve a murder shrouded in ancient Christian ritual. In Vladimir Nabokov's Lolita: An aging professor is obsessed with a troubled girl.

Let's go back to Mary and her mother.

"Who is Mary's mother? What's her name?"

"Her name is Adele," you say.

"And what does Adele want?"

"Adele has what she wants. She wants Mary to be dependent on her. She wants to keep her that way."

The problem with this story goal is that it is reactive. Adele doesn't have to do much except react to Mary when

Mary tries to free herself. This means that the entire story can easily be told from Mary's perspective. On the other hand, if Adele (who) wants to keep Mary at home so that she can control Mary's inheritance (what Adele wants), but Mary's uncle sees the ruse and is going to intervene (what's stopping Adele), Adele has a story goal. However, this story goal undermines Mary's story goal since Mary is not so helpless after all – her uncle is on her side. Be careful with an overabundance of characters and tangled story goals since they can quickly complicate matters, confuse the reader, and dilute the main storyline.

When writing a story goal, use present tense and consider what your protagonist wants and what's stopping him. The point of having a story goal is to stay focused and remind yourself in every sentence, paragraph, page, and scene what the story is about. Whenever you get stuck, review your story goal. This may hold the key. You may have strayed from the story goal or not defined the story goal well enough. Changing the story goal can change the entire trajectory of the story, and if you're well into the narrative, this could mean a substantial rewrite. Ugh. Anyway, a story goal propels the story. It defines the character, her wants, and what's stopping her, and it is the basis for the opening scene.

Opening scene. An opening scene illustrates the story goal. In the case of Mary and Adele, the first scene could be an argument between mother and daughter or a manipulation of the daughter by the mother. An opening scene should introduce the main character, present her dilemma and begin the forward trajectory by placing her off balance. Where and how a story opens is critical because that's when the reader gets hooked. No matter what kind of story you're telling – mystery, romance, science fiction, literary – the first sentence, paragraph, and page must have punch in clarity, tone, emotion, and conflict. There's no warming up, no meandering allowed.

To illustrate how stories start, here are a few opening sentences. Consider how they draw you in and the questions they raise. How clear is the story goal?

> Lolita, light of my life, fire of my loins. My sin, my soul. Lo-lee-ta: the tip of the tongue taking a trip of three steps down the palate to tap, at three, on the teeth. Lo. Lee. Ta
>
> -Lolita/Nabokov

> The story of Zenia ought to begin when Zenia began. It must have been someplace long ago and distant in space, thinks Tony; someplace bruised, and very tangled.
>
> -The Robber Bride/Atwood

> While Pearl Tull was dying, a funny thought occurred to her. It twitched her lips and rustled her breath, and she felt her son lean forward from where he kept watch by her bed. "Get ..." she told him. "You should have got ... "
>
> -Dinner at the Homesick Restaurant/Tyler

> On the afternoon of October 12, 1990, my twin brother Thomas entered the Three Rivers, Connecticut Public Library, retreated to one of the rear study carrels, and prayed to God the sacrifice he was about to commit would be deemed acceptable.
>
> -I Know This Much Is True/Lamb

In these short introductions, a reader is beautifully oriented. We are told who the story is about, whether the point of view (POV) character is in the first or third person, and given just enough information to keep us (or at least me) reading. The beginning of your story should start with action, a problem, or some punchy dialogue.

Point of View. What you may notice about these stories is that they are about the travails of one character. This is not an accident. A tighter, more riveting story will usually be told from one perspective or POV. Again, this reflects the human condition since we experience life from one perspective. The most common styles of POV are expressed in first person or third person subjective. Both these styles are limited to being inside a character's head, either in the I form, or the He/She/They form. The I form is a bit more constricting but intimate. The He/She/They form allows for more narrative, but there's also a distancing.

Refer to Story X. What POV style does your author use? Are there multiple POVs? If so, do they have their own story goals?

Tense. Just a brief word. When I first began writing, I struggled with tense. Most stories are written in the simple past – he ran, I thought, she wished – even though the story action is happening in the present. At first, this may seem jarring, but with practice, the use of past tense will become second nature. Tenses, generally, should not be mixed. I suspect this happens because we often use multiple tenses daily. Again, sticking with tense is easier the more one writes.

Vunderbar. Where are we now? We are writers with unique talents who write daily. We have a story goal, a POV character, and an idea for an opening scene that reflects the story goal. So are you off and running? Almost.

WATER THE SPROUT ~ PLOT

FILLING THIS EMPTY SPACE CONSTITUTES MY IDENTITY.
— TWYLA THARP

*B*ackstory...
 I was educated by an order of St. Joseph nuns who demanded outlines – those bewildering subsets of bulleted letters and numbers – for term papers. The concept of outlining was similar in my mind to looking up a word in the dictionary I didn't know how to spell. How could I outline when I didn't know the topic? So after I completed the assignment, I did the outline. Of course, the outline was supposed to be done before the report. But what was the point? I still had to write the darn thing. Anyway, I didn't come easily or willingly to the planning concept. No, that took me years of aimless writing.

My first manuscript was written after reading: See the scene as if it's on stage, watch what happens, then write it down. Brilliant, I could do that. And I did. However, the result was a meandering of the worst kind – backstory with no forward movement. So, where did I go wrong? Metaphorically speaking, I built a house without a blueprint.

"A blueprint? For a story?" you say. "But that's so contrived. What about the unpredictability of the characters? What about their freedom to express themselves untethered? Besides, you'll give too much away if you know the whole story. A story isn't a term paper. It's creative."

Yes, precisely; fiction is creative. Even more, it's boundless, it's imaginative, and it's where pumpkins turn into carriages. And it's precisely for these reasons that a general framework is needed. Stories do take on a life of their own. They can spiral out of control or drop like stones. Every innocent line of dialogue, narration, exposition, and description has the potential to draw the story off point. Sometimes you won't even realize it until you're pages ahead, pulling out your hair, wondering how events got so tangled, so lost.

I spent two years rewriting my first manuscript. Actually, I spent two years rewriting the first chapter of my first manuscript. Yes, I said the first chapter, two years. That's about as brainless as one can get. Naturally, during that time, I had serious questions about my sanity and writing ability. For some reason, the thought of planning the story never entered my consciousness. No, that came later, much later.

Eventually, I took on another story. This second manuscript had forward movement but ran out of steam on page 60. I had a general sense of where I was headed, but for some reason stopped cold. Ditto for two subsequent manuscripts. It wasn't until I was asked by a member of a writer's group to give him an idea of where the plot was going that I decided to put a brief narrative down on paper. Suddenly, the clouds cracked apart, and I understood what the nuns were asking.

Writers do a lot of thinking. In fact, we do more thinking than writing. Thoughts are lightning speed, transitory, winsome. And it is from these wild synaptic pulses that writers attempt to fashion a comprehensible story. Writing fiction is also a creative process of honing, shaving, twisting, and turning ideas. It's first brainstorming, then funneling down. It's evaluating and deciding. Fiction breathes, grows, and mutates before becoming a finished story. In the process, some sorting out needs to happen.

There is no right or wrong way to blueprint a story since it is a working document designed by you for you. Conceptualizing a story can grow from listing possible climatic moments to pages of chapter summaries. The format can be a narrative, in bullets, flow charts, on cards, or a combination of all of the above. It is important to write down some outline rather than leave it swimming amorphously in the head, where it can be forgotten or overwritten.

So, where does a writer begin? We'll start with plot.

The plot is what happens in the story, and your characters make things happen. In other words, characters drive the action. Story is also about conflict, and the purveyors of that conflict are the characters. As in real life, what mainly defines us is not how we look or where we were born but our reactions to life events, struggles, and successes. A new mother and a soldier back from war are both qualitatively changed. Likewise, place your main character in an ocean with sharks, and how does he respond? What does this tell you about the man?

Robert McKee, the author of Story, defines conflict areas in storytelling. Besides inner conflict, there are personal conflicts with family, lovers, friends, and extra-personal conflicts with the physical environment, social institutions, and other individuals. Specifically, conflict in a character's world can be with a father, a company, or a hurricane. At every stage in your story, conflict must be an exterior problem that relentlessly plays on your star. Seeing how your protagonist reacts makes up his character. Therefore, when considering a plot outline, consider the conflict your protagonist is facing.

Let's go back to Mary and her mother, Adele. The story goal is about a girl named Mary who wants to be out of her mother's home and away from her mother's controlling ways, but she doesn't have the means or the confidence to leave. With this in mind, how will the conflict between these two forces play out? Answer this question by brainstorming. Write down whatever comes to mind, where anything is possible. Here's my list:

- Adele puts Mary down. Doesn't like the way she dresses or her cooking.

- Adele makes fun of Mary. Says she takes after Mary's father.

- Adele embarrasses Mary by trying to set Mary up at a church social with an old widower, a plan that is doomed to fail.

- Mary doesn't defend herself directly but is passive-aggressive.

- Mary overeats. Doesn't eat. Avoids being with mother.

- Mary pretends to be someone else. Meets a man online.

- After an incident at church, Mary becomes incensed.

- Mary tries to get away by joining the army.

- Adele plans to kill Mary if she leaves.

Brainstorming is not about making sense. Just place thoughts down on paper, and stop when you run out of ideas. Do this a few times, and you'll have a treasure trove of conflict . . . and more.

The process of brainstorming is expansive and associative. For example, when I considered the conflict between Mary and Adele, I also thought of a scenario, a line of dialogue, or a place. In the list above, Mary's father came up twice. This theme could be explored more. With the story goal in mind, I could then brainstorm another question. How does the father dynamic affect the conflict between mother and daughter?

- Adele always felt the father loved Mary more.

- Mary misses her father and stays in the house to be close to the memories.

- Mary looks like her father.

- Adele allowed the father to leave but would not let Mary walk out.

- Adele will never be lonely again.

Whenever you want to expand on an item in the list, consider asking Wh questions, such as Why does Mary feel this way? What is Adele's motivation? Where is the father? If Mary does X, what will Adele do? The only restriction is always to keep the story goal in mind.

Evaluating the list comes next. Will you use all the ideas? No. Mark those that appeal to you. Then, with the shortlist, put the ideas in some order. Next, map out conflict or plot points (what happens) that build toward the climax or show-down scene. For example, if Adele tries to kill Mary, this would be the showdown scene. The sooner you know the showdown scene, the easier it is to plan your story. A rough draft of conflict and potential scenes may be all that's needed to begin writing. Congratulations! Not only do you have a blueprint, but you've learned a process that will serve you well. Brainstorming is fun and can be utilized at every level of storytelling.

Having spent some time with Adele and Mary, we're now ready to tackle three other types of outlines: Demographics, Timelines, Research.

Demographics. Characters' names, ages, occupations, and what they look like are a few of the demographics that can be outlined. Putting this information in a clear and easily refer- enced format will help avoid continuity problems throughout the story. Tip: In coming up with a character's looks, I think of a real person en toto. For example, I may see a character as a Brad Pitt type so that whenever I refer to the character, I'll have the same characteristics in mind – slender build, blue eyes.

Timeline. What is the time frame of the story? Does the story transpire in days, years, or a lifetime? When does the story begin? Timelines specify the time of day, the day of the week, the month, and the year. Another consideration could be the seasons. Once again, the sooner you get a handle on the story's timeline, the fewer continuity problems you'll have. If not done from the outset, recreating a timeline can be tedious at best. While critical to every story, not all time-lines are created equally. A contemporary story may only need general references to time, but the time element in a mystery or a historical novel plays an integral role. The time frame must be precise if you want to set up suspects/alibis or anchor the narrative in actual events.

Research. No matter what kind of story you're telling, research is inevitable. With plot, character, and time in mind, you should be reasonably aware of what needs to be researched. However, before going off on unnecessary tangents, utilize what you already know—places you've visited, jobs you've had—and incorporate this first-hand knowledge into the story. Family, friends, and acquaintances may provide a treasure trove of information from the lives they've led. Be curious and ask questions. Since I write contemporary fiction, I research as I write. Naturally, the Internet is tremendously helpful. Utilize search engines like Google and Yahoo. Besides keywords, explore images, videos, and maps. Should you come across an informative article and want to learn more, consider emailing the author. It's important to remember, however, that research is a back-drop, and story is a character struggling.

With outline in hand, consider the following questions:

Does the story begin with change? If you are warming up to the story – giving background, describing the sunset, documenting a dull day in life – step back and look for an event that throws your POV character off guard. How the story begins is critical in getting a reader hooked.

Is there too little or too much story? An outline will give you the sense if you have too little or too much story. The best time to deal with either problem is during the outline phase. Once the story is underway, major adjustments to expand or condense translate into a monumental headache.

To beef up a book, consider adding another level of conflict for the POV character. Let's go back to Mary and her mother, Adele. Besides the dilemma that Mary has with her controlling mother, maybe Mary is also obsessed with a man she met online. Tossing in a secondary conflict adds a subplot. So how many subplots should you consider? Be careful. Each subplot must be resolved and shouldn't overpower the main conflict.

Conversely, if your story is overly complicated to outline, focus on the story goal, reduce the number of characters, and shear down the subplots.

Are there twists? Turns in the story can happen in both small and large ways. Good storytelling is a delicate balancing act, an interplay of what is known and not known, what is familiar and not familiar. An outline provides an overview of the story; the more you know, the more you can surprise and delight the reader. Again, go to that favorite book of yours. How did the author keep your attention? What, if anything, made the story seem stale?

Does the end of your story resolve the story goal? If the story goal isn't addressed by the end, there's a problem. Nobody likes a bait and switch. It's also preferable to have a definitive ending where there's closure. I think endings correlate more directly with reader satisfaction than any other element. Of course, the reader must get to the last page to have this happen.

"Enough," you say. "Let's get on with the writing."

"Yes. Let's."

TEND THE BLOOM ~ SCENE

I TRY TO LEAVE OUT THE PARTS THAT PEOPLE SKIP.
— ELMORE LEONARD

a written story is magical. And writers who write stories are wizards of the highest order. Here we sit, placing symbols on a page that somehow, remarkably, without actors or music or sound effects or even the spoken word, infuse a storyline replete with images and emotions into a reader's mind and heart. How is this possible? Well, like magic, it's trickery, plain and simple. For a moment, let's step back and remember our communal past.

I suspect most of us got the writing bug from reading other people's stories. Stories that made our eyes fly over the lines, made us turn the pages, made our hearts pound, made us worry and wonder and laugh and cry. Such is the power of a story. It ropes us in, then wraps around two basic human traits: emotion and curiosity. When a reader feels or is desperate to know more, that's when we have succeeded. Such a conjuring feat begins with the basics where the top hat and rabbit are Scene and Sequel, and the wand is Cause and Effect.

Scene. The scene is the basic indivisible unit of fiction where the action plays out, forces collide, and emotions ebb and flow. Delectably distasteful but true, scene is also a manipulation of the reader. To pull this off, the writer must be aware of the hidden purpose of the scene. The following questions will lead the way with the story goal in mind.

-Who's in the scene? When considering the number of characters in a scene, "Less is more" should be a constant refrain. Conflict is portrayed and heightened with more clarity and punch when there are two, and only two, opposing characters. Conversely, when more characters are roaming around, the writer runs the risk of diluting the struggle or confusing the reader, faultlines that, once rattled, can stop the reader from reading.

-What does each character want? This is where conflict plays out. While you may be in one character's POV, it is essential to know each character's agenda, for then they can dodge and lunge attacks. Conflict is an interchange where gains are made, then lost; a two-steps-forward-three-steps-back scenario.

-How does each character feel? Whenever I write, I always identify how each character is feeling. Why? So I can change it. If a character is bored, by the end of the scene, I'll have her engaged. If a character is happy, I'll make her sad. This type of manipulation has tremendous payoffs. For one, it makes change occur. Change, a shift in the status quo, is essential in a scene. Secondly, emotional content hooks a reader and heightens the drama. The only caveat is to express one emotional state at a time. In other words, don't make a character actively lonely and angry, and vengeful. Instead, decide on one emotion that then changes to another.

-What's the outcome? Resolution of the scene is the gasp.

Here someone loses, usually your protagonist. When deciding on an outcome, play around with a few options.

Returning to Mary and Adele, let's do a scene outline of Characters, Objectives, Emotions, and Outcomes.

-Characters: Mary and Adele

-Objectives: Mary wants to stay home so she can go online and instant message a man she recently met. Adele wants Mary to go to church.

-Emotions: Mary is anxious for her mother to leave. The computer is in the corner of the living room. Adele is angry that Mary won't go to church. Adele also knows about the man online. Adele has planned to have Mary meet a man at church instead.

-Outcome: Mary reluctantly agrees to attend church after Adele has a "spell." Adele's spells always occur when she feels there's no other way to manipulate Mary.

Sequel. I first read about sequel in Jack Bickham's Scene and Structure, a book every fiction writer should own, never lend out, and revere. We are not worthy. Sequel occurs after a scene. It's when your POV character stands back, processes what has happened, and decides on a course of action. By nature, a sequel moves the plot forward, tantalizes the reader, slows the pace, and provides a transition. All are tools that will make your story controllable, interesting, and seamless. A sequel can be as short as a sentence or as long as a chapter.

-Move the plot forward. While scene is action, sequel is thought. Think of a day in your life. On your way to work, a car runs a red light at the intersection you are driving through. You slam on the brakes and close your eyes, knowing that impact will happen. Remarkably, with your heart exploding inside your chest, the sports car speeds past. You are stunned but unscathed. So, do you drive away? Possibly, but not without thinking about what a jerk that guy was and your next course of action. Should you call 911? Follow him? Find out where he lives so you can move next door and torment him with chipmunk music twenty-four hours a day. In the sequel, you explore and expound on your protagonist's reaction to a situation.

-Entice the reader. Movies have trailers, those sound bites, and clips that hopefully catch your attention. Sequels in fiction do a similar job. They give the reader a little tease of what's to come. Suddenly, you take a hard left and follow the punk . . . then end the chapter.

-Slow the pace. The sequel is telling. And telling slows the plot. So whenever you have a particularly emotional scene, quiet it down with a longer sequel. In a sequel, you can have your POV character puzzle over clues, character's motives, etc.

-Provide a transition. Sequel provides a segue: a link between scenes. Sequels are connective tissue that can appear anywhere in the story when a character processes what has just happened. A chapter may have many scenes with short sequels between them. No need to rack your brain wondering how your protagonist will exit the room. Simply have her react, think, plan, then end the scene.

Consider presenting sequel in the order of emotion to thought to decision.

Emotion. How is your character feeling? Feeling is a gut reaction and usually comes before conscious thought. You can tell the reader how the character feels, or you can describe his reactions. Description can also mirror feelings.

Thought. Once the feeling is expressed, what does your character think? A character's thought can be expressed through dialogue, action or interior thought.

Decision. What does your character decide? What's his next course of action? This can be shown by action, dialogue or thoughts.

A sequel for Mary and Adele may play out like this:

Mary followed behind her mother. At the front door, she turned and looked back at the computer. Weak-kneed, she felt sick to her stomach (emotion). Would he understand that she had to go to church? Of course. If he loved her, truly loved her (thought). Mary glanced at the wall clock. The church service was only forty-five minutes. She could rush back while her mother stayed for cake and coffee (decision). Yes, he'd understand. She'd convince him.

End scene, then show Mary and Adele at church.

Cause and Effect. The scene followed by the sequel illustrates the basic principle of cause and effect, where your POV character reacts to what just happened. Such causal relationships loop throughout the story and lend fiction believability. Unlike life, events in a story have to happen for a reason—no deus ex machina (acts of God).

But scene and sequel are just one such causal relationship. Cause and effect occur at every level of a story's construction, from sentence to paragraph to page to chapter. A give-and-take conversation, an explanation of action, and interior thoughts must all follow this sequence. So when a story becomes confusing, it's usually due to a cause-and-effect problem. And when a reader is confused, they stop reading, and when a reader stops reading, that's a very, very bad thing.

Cause and effect is the internal integrity of the story, the thread that pulls the vivid, continuous dream through the eye of the needle. This concept provides a logical framework, forward motion, and continuity. No small feat for such a fundamental principle. But you have to be careful. It's not so easy or so clear. In fact, cause and effect can become quite muddled.

A written story is comprised of lines of words that must follow each other in a one-dimensional medium. Therefore, when parts are left out or not in the proper order, the story fragments.

Problems occur when: cause has no effect, effect has no cause, effect precedes cause, and last but not least, there is simultaneous cause and effect. These problems can be found at every level of the story and are not something any word-processing program can find. This creates a dilemma.

-Cause with no effect. A cause without an effect occurs when an event happens for no particular reason or without effect. Naturally, a scene without a sequel would qualify, as well as tangential meanderings that stray from the story goal. But causal relationships also exist on a smaller scale. Consider this line: He flipped the switch and looked into her cold blue eyes. What is the effect of flipping the switch? Looking into her cold eyes? To follow cause and effect it should read: He flipped the switch. Light flooded the room. He looked into her cold blue eyes.

-Effect with no cause. This scenario is usually the starting point for a mystery. A dead body is the effect of some unspecified cause, i.e., murder, suicide. But it also occurs when some critical cause or event happens outside the purview of the story. This is not a problem if your POV character is likewise in the dark. However, if your POV character withholds information that is later divulged, this can lead to some nasty reviews. Artful manipulation of a reader is one thing, but playing him for a fool is quite another. Effect with no cause is the culprit when a POV character acts or reacts for no apparent reason. Sometimes the cause exists, but it is too far removed from the effect. Whenever a reader is left wondering why, effect with no cause may be the problem.

-Effect precedes cause. When an effect precedes cause, it can be jarring. The following sentences illustrate this problem: He shot three times after pulling out the gun, or Larry crumpled to the floor when the bullet hit. The proper sequence calls for cause to precede effect. After pulling out the gun, he shot three times, or When the bullet hit, Larry crumpled to the floor. When sentences are choppy or difficult to follow, the effect preceding the cause may be the problem.

-Simultaneous cause and effect. Writers often use certain constructions – as, "ing" verbs – to relate simultaneous cause and effect. This becomes problematic when such sentences don't make sense. An example: Ripping off the sheet, she collapsed onto the bed. This sentence implies that two events are happening simultaneously, which, when imagined, seems unlikely. A better-stated sentence is: She ripped off the sheet and collapsed onto the bed. It is always better to write clearly than take shortcuts by combining phrases that may or may not make sense. Simultaneous cause and effect are more easily expressed when one type of modality, such as thought, causes an effect in a different modality, such as action. For instance: With her silence playing on his mind, he slammed the cupboard door. Simultaneity problems arise when several characters in a scene are actively speaking, thinking, and doing.

The principle of cause and effect seems obvious, but it isn't. When something doesn't make sense in our work, it's usually because the causal relationship has been compromised.

Now that we have taken a look at the hidden magic that goes into writing scenes, let's turn our attention to the magic that is out in the open.

FILL THE GARDEN ~ DEVELOPMENT

EVERYTHING YOU CAN IMAGINE IS REAL.
— PABLO PICASSO

*a*t last, we're in the trenches, armed and ready to meet the challenge of putting it all together. Here's where we discuss the nuts and bolts of fiction – how to present the story.

Consider the following elements:

1) Action
2) Interior thought
3) Emotional content
4) Description
5) Dialogue
6) Exposition

Depending on the genre and your particular sensibilities, you may be more heavy-handed in one element. For instance, science fiction or romance may have more description. Literary fiction may have more internal thought. When I write a story, I mix these elements. This is considered a commercial style. An example follows:

In the middle of slicing onions, the phone rang. Marnie took a few steps and glanced at the caller ID. Tina. Marnie shook her head and went back to the cutting board.

The answering machine clicked on. "I know you're there. This is important. Really important."

Marnie glared at the phone. She wasn't going to bite. Everything with her sister was catastrophic from the time they were little, such a drama queen.

"It's about that husband of yours. Pick up the damn phone."

Now let's define and discuss the elements.

Action: In the middle of slicing onions, the phone rang. Marnie took a few steps and glanced at the caller ID.

Action occurs when a character is doing something. It's what you'd see if the scene were on stage or at the movies. Action is external. Snippets of action, like the one above, orient the reader by anchoring the character in a place, time, and situation. Longer stretches of action, called dramatic action, heighten the tension. Dramatic action occurs when something happens, and your POV character is in the middle. To dramatize action, add detail. If the action is only to orient the reader, keep it simple and direct. In other words, don't get caught up in how Marnie is holding the onion.

Interior Thought: Tina.

Interior thought is what your POV character thinks. Thoughts can be expressed in incomplete sentences, questions, or long paragraphs. Interior thought is the one element that is unique to written fiction. Thoughts play a critical role in the cause-and-effect sequence. Besides being used in sequel, thoughts are utilized throughout the narrative in linking all the other elements. Effective thoughts precipitate change. In the example above, the thought, Tina, causes Marnie to shake her head, a subtle reaction or change.

Thoughts are punctuated in many ways, i.e., italicized OR done in plain text with a tag of "he thought" OR written in incomplete sentences OR paragraphed on their own. However you choose to punctuate, be consistent and don't mix the different formats. Thoughts are never placed within quotes of any kind.

Emotional Content: Marnie shook her head and went back to the cutting board.

As I stated earlier, a character's feelings should always be known so that you can play them with wild abandon. This goes for all the characters in the scene. When illustrating emotional content, think of an approaching train. Begin with a distant rumbling that then builds as the scene continues. Emotional content can be shown by what a character does, says, senses, or thinks. In this example, it's tucked inside a character's action. Later with the sentence, She glared at the phone, the emotional tenor is raised a notch.

Description: The machine clicked on.

Description is what is sensed (i.e., seen, smelled, touched, heard, tasted). Sensory detail brings vividness into the reader's mind. And the more specific the detail, the better. Again, when writing description, consider the emotional state of your characters. What you describe should mirror the emotional content, thus establishing a mood. I began the above paragraph with, In the middle of slicing onions, the phone rang, but what if I'd started with, In the middle of licking an ice cream cone, the phone rang? Which description mirrors the mood of the scene better? Even the most seemingly inconsequential description makes a difference. Description of place is called setting. When writing about a place, try to go there. What are the sounds, smells? How does the light change? When choosing detail, make it unique. A windy beach with white caps is good, but blowing sand that stings his cheek is better.

Dialogue: "I know you're there. This is important. Really important."

Written dialogue is different from spoken dialogue. Everyday communication is mundane, roundabout. Story dialogue is clipped and gets to the heart of the matter. Dialogue is the main vehicle used for expressing conflict. Some basic Do's:

– Do use contractions and sentence fragments.

– Do use punctuation instead of a tag. For example, "Get out of here!"

– Do consider who's talking, i.e., a child should not sound like a university professor.

– Do use tags other than said sparingly, e.g., he demanded, she cooed.

– Do follow cause and effect:

Not so good: "Where's John? He owes me money."

"To the store."

Better: "John owes me money. Where'd he go?"

"To the store."

– Do use an em-dash at the end of a line of dialogue to denote an interruption.

"It's your father again. He yelled about the dinner. I told him to— "

"Mom, please. Let's talk about something else."

– Do use an ellipsis to denote a trailing off.

"I stopped at Chin's for some take-out. Frank was there. He looked . . ."

"Looked how?"

Exposition: Everything with her sister was catastrophic from when they were little, such a drama queen.

In fiction, exposition is background information that addresses underlying reasons for current actions, feelings, and thoughts. It's a form of telling that stops forward movement. In commercial fiction, it's best presented in snippets. If an event in a character's history is crucial to the story, consider starting the story from that particular event then move forward in time. Exposition can be paragraphed or woven into dialogue, description or interior thought. Exposition must have a purpose. Leave it out if it's filler information – where your character was born.

Utilizing these elements will keep the narrative moving along. When you're stuck, read your last written sentence, then ask, in response, what is the character doing (action), thinking (internal thought), feeling (emotional content), sensing (description), saying (dialogue)? And why (exposition)? When you think of writing this way, you will automatically do what writing books expound upon: showing, telling, and following cause with effect.

Two other concepts will help make a scene exciting and seamless: Pacing and Transitions.

-Pacing. Part of the magic of a good book is how the book is paced. Like many other aspects, pacing occurs in varying forms and levels throughout the story. Alternating the main plot with a subplot can give an ebb and flow to the narrative. But there are other pacing tools. Scene speeds pace, sequel slows it down. Stretches of exposition, description, and interior thought decelerate the scene, but dialogue and dramatic summary rev it to breakneck speed. Short staccato sentences are fast. Long sentences are slow. Also, to prevent the rhythm from becoming stilted, rearrange the placement of the subject, verb, and object and sandwich short sentences between longer ones.

-Transitions. Sequels provide a transition from one scene to another, but there are times when you need to move along the story continuum without having a sequel. You'll often see a double drop space to denote a change of time or place, but seamless transitions can be applied using Emotion, Weather, Dialogue, Name, and Time.

-Emotion: He was angry. So angry he'd blow her head off. By the time the police came, he was still angry.

-Weather: The hail pelted against the window. When the sun came out, he headed for the barn.

-Dialogue: He'd have to talk to her.

"What do you want?" she said through the crack in the door.

-Name: Clearly, the missing link was Kara in Apartment 3C. She was taller than he imagined. And not so young.

-Time: Two days later, the phone still hadn't rung.

WONDERFUL! You now have all the building blocks to write fiction. Did I leave out anything? Hmm . . .

Oh, yeah, there's the part that makes a writer dash up five flights of stairs, throw open the window, and jump.

DIG THE WEEDS ~ REWRITE

I BELIEVE MORE IN THE SCISSORS THAN I DO IN THE PENCIL.
— TRUMAN CAPOTE

*V*isualize . . .

With the Dom Pérignon chilling and dinner guests about to arrive, I fan the manuscript pages. I'm amazed, shocked, and awed by the lines and lines of beautifully typed words. Such a sense of achievement. I then turn to page one, the opening scene I'll read after supper, and mouth each word.

In the hallway, the clock strikes seven. Each gong is unnerving. Each gong, as I read, is alarming. Suddenly, the doorbell rings. My body jerks, electrified. Guests are arriving. But something is amiss. The words and the sentences are all wrong: typos, misspellings, adverbs, were's, and was's. Such nonsense! The bell is insistent and accusatory. There's only one way out. I jump to the dining table, grab a fork, then dive to the nearest wall plug . . .

Alas, what was once written must be written again and again and again. It's an inevitable and frustrating endeavor that also offers a tremendous opportunity for growth. With each problem faced, each sentence tweaked, and each word replaced by another, your writing will improve, and mistakes will hopefully not be made again. An independent writer must learn how to evaluate and correct their work. Yes, editing services can be purchased, but they do not come cheaply.

The review of your work should go from the general to the specific, namely: Diagnostic Read, Line-by-Line Editing, and Copyediting.

Diagnostic Read. Once your manuscript is finished, have someone read it. But who? Perhaps someone in your writer's group or someone who reads a lot. Someone who you can reasonably trust and who'll be honest. Getting feedback can be frustrating since the evaluation of a manuscript is subjective. Also, this is not the time to develop thin skin and get defensive. Whatever the response, try to evaluate its validity with a clear mind. If many readers identify the same issues, you should take their comments under strong advisement and consideration. Ask readers the following questions that may provide clues to problematic areas:

Questions to ask, followed by problem areas to address concerns.

Were you confused at any point?

Problem area: Something was either left out, glossed over, or too many things were happening at once. An overabundance of characters. Cause and effect problems.

Did something not make sense?

Problem area: Tangential events strayed from the story goal. Not enough or unclear information was given to the reader. Facts were incorrect. Illogical motivation.

Were you bored?

Problem area: Conflict was not developed. Emotional content was flat. Forward movement stalled. Too many irrelevant details. Too many flashbacks. Slow start. Boring characters.

Was something missing?

Problem area: Underdeveloped or unresolved storyline and subplots. Lack of vividness.

A change, such as adding or deleting a scene, can cause a domino effect. That's why it's important to have a working outline from the outset. Still, whatever is broken can be fixed. Relax. Take each problem and work it out.

Line-by-Line Editing. Line-by-line editing is where you read each sentence and evaluate its efficacy and proper use of the English language. Line-by-line editing is the time to sit down, get comfortable, and read every sentence carefully. Two reference books to have on hand are a dictionary and William Strunk's The Elements of Style.

Below you'll find a line-by-line edit I did on the first paragraph of this book. A discussion follows of why I made the changes.

Before line-by-line: I'm standing before you, a decidedly middle-aged woman, round, doughy and blinking through smudged glasses. It's six p.m. We are in a VFW Post drinking bitter coffee from Styrofoam cups. I look worried and I am. It's my turn to disclose. All eyes, expectant, are on me. I clear my throat, swallow and say, "My name is Linda . . ." I pause, unsure if I should proceed. What will you think? That I'm a fool, a loser? I want to run, but I've come this far. Instead, I steady myself and blurt out the words, ". . . and I'm self-published."

After line-by-line: Before you I stand,1 a decidedly middle-aged woman, round, doughy, and blinking through smudged glasses. It's six p.m. We're2 in a VFW Post drinking bitter coffee from Styrofoam cups. I'm worried.3 It's my turn to disclose. All eyes, expectant, are on me. I clear my throat, swallow, 4 then say, "My name is Linda — "5 I stop cold.6

What will you think? That I'm a fool, a loser? I want to run, but I've come this far. My confession tumbles out.7 "And I'm self-published." 8

Reasoning:

1. In the first sentence, a decidedly middle-aged woman, follows the word you. One could assume then that you are a decidedly middle-aged woman. To correct this, I rearranged the starting prepositional phrase so that the qualifying phrase is clearly about me.

2. We are changed to We're. A conversation style sets an intimate tone.

3. I look worried, and I am; changed to I'm worried. First person faux pas. How can I look at myself without a mirror?

4. and changed to then. Clearer progression. Less simultaneous action.

5. "My name is Linda . . ." changed to "My name is Linda —" Ellipsis denote a trailing off, an em-dash, an abrupt interruption. I made this change after I made a change in the following sentence.

6. I pause, unsure if I should proceed, changed to I stop cold—more punch, action, and decisiveness.

7. Instead, I steady myself and blurt out the words, changed to My confession tumbles out—cleaner and crisper.

8. ". . . and I'm self-published." changed to "And I'm self-published." Ellipses denote a trailing off and are used at the end of a line of dialogue.

As illustrated, every sentence can be a minefield. The above changes were made after I tweaked the paragraph many times. Line-by-line editing is subjective, and I suspect no two writers or editors would make the same changes. Still, there are many common mistakes:

- Redundant nouns, pronouns, verbs, and phrases.
- Overuse of passive voice construction: was, were.

- Overuse of adverbs (ly verb), infinitives (to+verb), and present participles (ing verb)
- Cliches.
- Complicated tense as in the past perfect, had to, have had to, had to have been.
- Metaphors/similes that miss the mark.
- Simultaneous action. As/While construction.
- Profanity.
- Cause and effect problems.
- Continuity issues, i.e., Jimmie in one place, Jimmy in another.
- Weird sentences that, quite frankly, make no sense.

Copyediting. Copyediting is more trawling for errant punctuation and the minutiae of misspellings, misplaced, misused, or just plain missing words. There are many tools in your word processing program to help. Begin with spelling and grammar checkers. While these tools are not foolproof, they will always find pesky little typos, and you may even learn a thing or two: Foreign words are italicized. Brand names are capitalized. Numerals inside dialogue are always spelled out except for years.

Another godsend is the Find and Replace function. This function searches any word. For example, if your writing has an overabundance of a verb, looked, you can begin a search and replace them with other verbs. Besides redundancies, here's a list of some words that I often check to see if they're used properly:

-your, you're
-their, there, they're
-lie, lay (present and past tense of to lie)
-lay, laid (present and past tense of to lay)
-that, which (see The Elements of Style)
-farther (distance), further (time or quantity). The boy threw the ball farther.

You can even search keystrokes. For example: . " (period followed by an extra space and end quote).

After the trials of missing a bevy of typos and putting out a second edition of my first novel, I've come upon many helpful techniques and apps. First, read the story backward. Yes, it sounds overwhelming, but it's quite effective. Reading copy from the last word to the first allows you to focus on specific words, phrases, and sentences rather than be besotted by overly read text where blind spots abound. Second, have the story read back to you with the text-to-speech function on most computers or writing apps. Third, invest in an editing app. While not free, they are a time saver if you plan on writing a lot.

FINAL THOUGHTS

*S*uch is my take on creative writing. Please understand this is not a definitive book on writing fiction since writing is an innovative, expansive process. Still, I hope you have found *On Creative Writing* helpful.

Thirty years ago, I dreamed of writing the great American novel. That dream remains, but another came true. I am a writer.

GUIDELINES FOR A WRITER'S GROUP

Sign-in sheet. Depending on the group size, order preference
will be given to those who haven't read the prior session.
A writer will have a set amount of time, i.e., fifteen minutes,
to present their unpublished work. Pieces can be read aloud
or silently. Members are encouraged to write comments on
handouts. All handouts will be returned to the author unless
otherwise arranged.

- Depending on the genre of writing, consider the following
areas to critique:

Fiction:
Opening, Conflict, Plot, Setting, Characterization,
Dialogue, Point of View, Showing, Telling, Format,
Grammar, Spelling, Style.

Poetry:
Subject, Title, Form, Structure, Rhyme, Meter,
Layout, Line Breaks, Rhythm, Cliches, Imagery, Vocabu-
lary, Adjectives, Adverbs, Showing, Telling.

Non-Fiction:

Structure, Argument, Topic, Readability,

Illustrations, Anecdotes, Accuracy, References, Grammar, Spelling, Title.

- Critiques of work will follow. All members are encouraged to participate, but can also PASS if they have no comment.

- During critiquing, the critiquing member has the floor. Critiques should not be more than five minutes.

- After the critiques, the author responds, and a general discussion follows.

BIBLIOGRAPHY

Atwood, M. (1993). The Robber Bride. New York: Bantam Books.

Bickham, J. (1993). Scene & Structure. Cincinnati: Writer's Digest Books.

Gardner, J. (1983). The Art of Fiction. Notes on Craft for Young Writers. New York:Vintage.

Lamb, W. (1998). I Know This Much Is True. New York: HarperCollins.

McKee, R. (1997). Story. New York: ReganBooks

Nabokov, V. (1955). Lolita. New York: Random House.

Strunk, W., Jr., & White, E. B. (1979). The Elements of Style. New York: Macmillian.

Tyler, A. (1982). Dinner at the Homesick Restaurant. New York: Ivy Books.

ABOUT THE AUTHOR

Award-winning writer and artist, Linda A Lavid, lives in Western New York with familiars of the human and animal variety. She is particularly fond of dried flowers, crinkly and pale, that collect dust in empty jars. According to Linda, they tell stories of lives memorialized in brittle repose of our eternal journey.

ALSO BY LINDA A LAVID

HOWIE IN LOVE: A HATTIE MOON MYSTERY

MURDER IN THE PACHYSANDRA: A HATTIE MOON MYSTERY

PALOMA: A LAURENT & DOVE MYSTERY

IF FLOWERS WERE CAKE: AND OTHER COLLAGES (ART/STORIES)

THE SIMPLE MECHANIC OF INFINITE EXECUTION (NOVELLA)

BLOOD ON THE PAGE (NOVELLA)

THE DYING OF ED MEES (NOVELLA)

OBITS FOR FUN: ILLUSTRATED REVIEWS FOR THOSE DEPARTED (HUMOR)

101 WAYS TO MEDITATE: DISCOVER YOUR TRUE SELF

101 MANERAS DE MEDITAR: DESCUBRA SU VERDADERO YO

ON CREATIVE WRITING

SOBRE ESCRITURA CREATIVA

RENTED ROOMS (SHORT FICTION)

OF THE DANCE/DE LA DANZA (SHORT FICTION/DUAL LANGUAGE)

CATS: WINSOME & WISE (ART)

WOMAN & FLIGHT (ART)

MUJER Y VUELO (ART/SPANISH)